Dear Fellow Artist,

Thank you for coming along on this visual arts journey with me. In the following pages I am excited to share my-crazy-self with you, for each piece is an original hand drawn J.B. McKracken design.

This book was designed to allow you the opportunity to remove your finished work for preservation. In addition, you can color multi-page original designs and then put each piece together to create a larger piece. Both can be done without compromising the integrity of any other design.

I truly hope that you have fun, happy times while creating your original J.B. McKracken designs. Again, thank you for taking this visual adventure with me.

Best Wishes,

Jay Bird McKracken

About the Artist

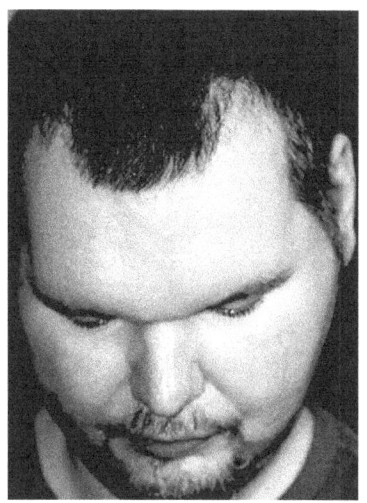

JB McKracken was born in January 1976 in Central Indiana.   Within his first two years it was discovered that JB had a genetic neuromuscular disease that was going to hinder his independence for life.

From the beginning, JB always had an interest in visual arts. Spending hours at a time drawing and painting at his home, JB developed an appreciation for self-expression at a young age. However, throughout his early years he noticed changes in his strength and it became more difficult for JB to use traditional methods to develop his art. This is when he began to experiment and seek out new methods of expression.

Presently JB continues his artistic quest for expression in Indiana. Creating all of time is his life elixir feeding his drive to share himself with the world.

MULTI-PAGE ARTWORK

Title: Bish

2014

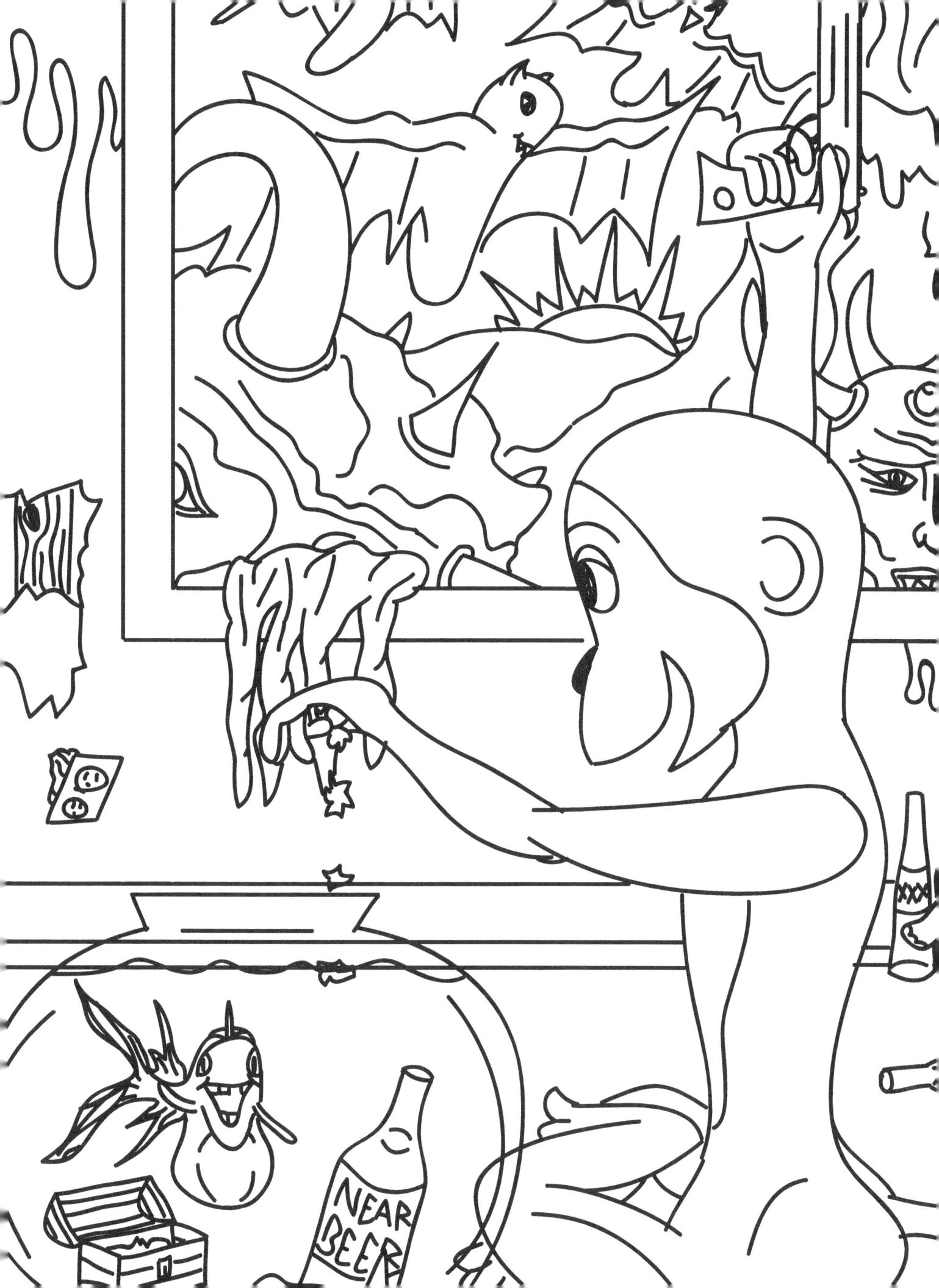

MULTI-PAGE ARTWORK

Title: Bish

2014

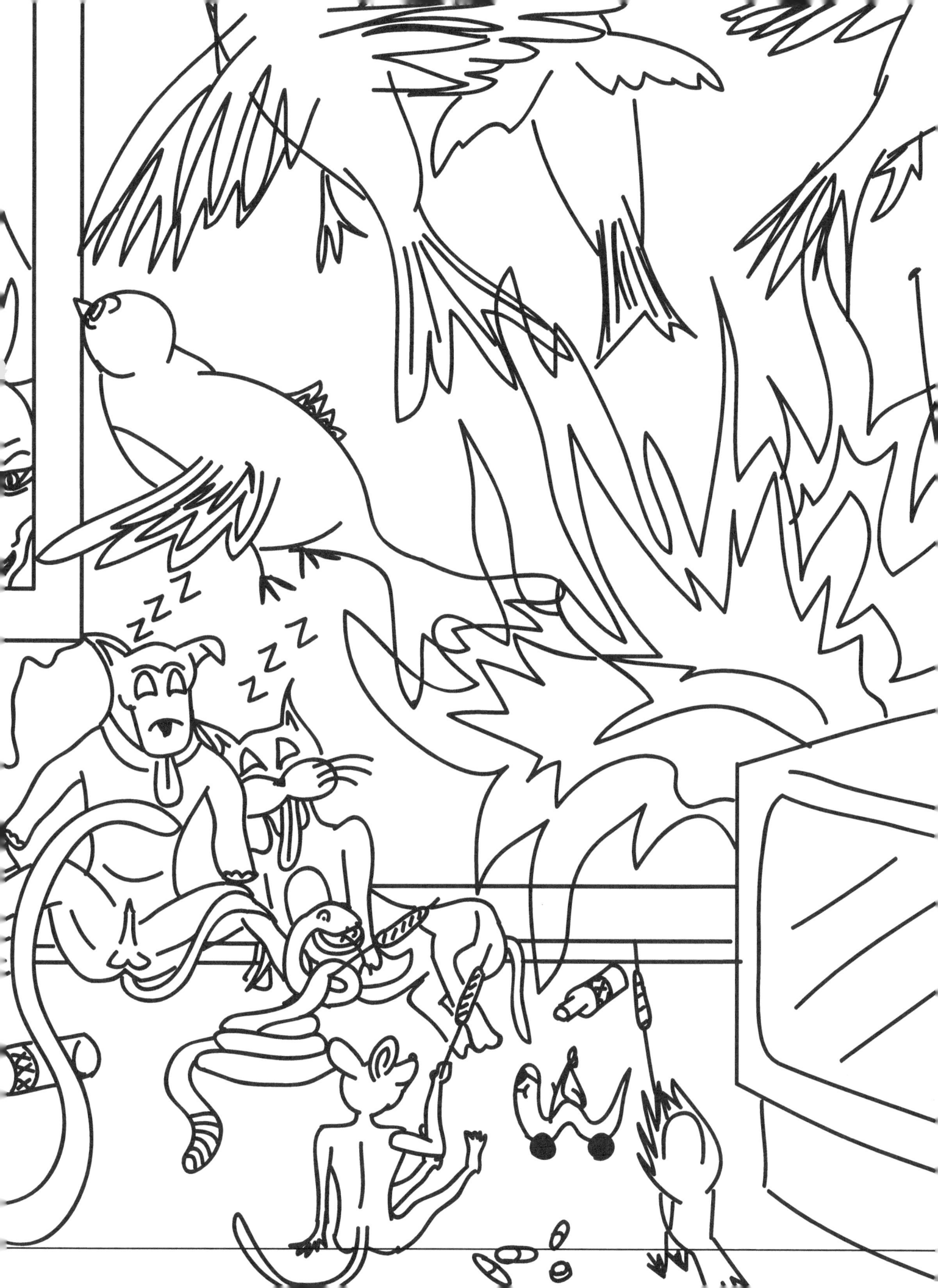

MULTI-PAGE ARTWORK

Title: Bish
2014

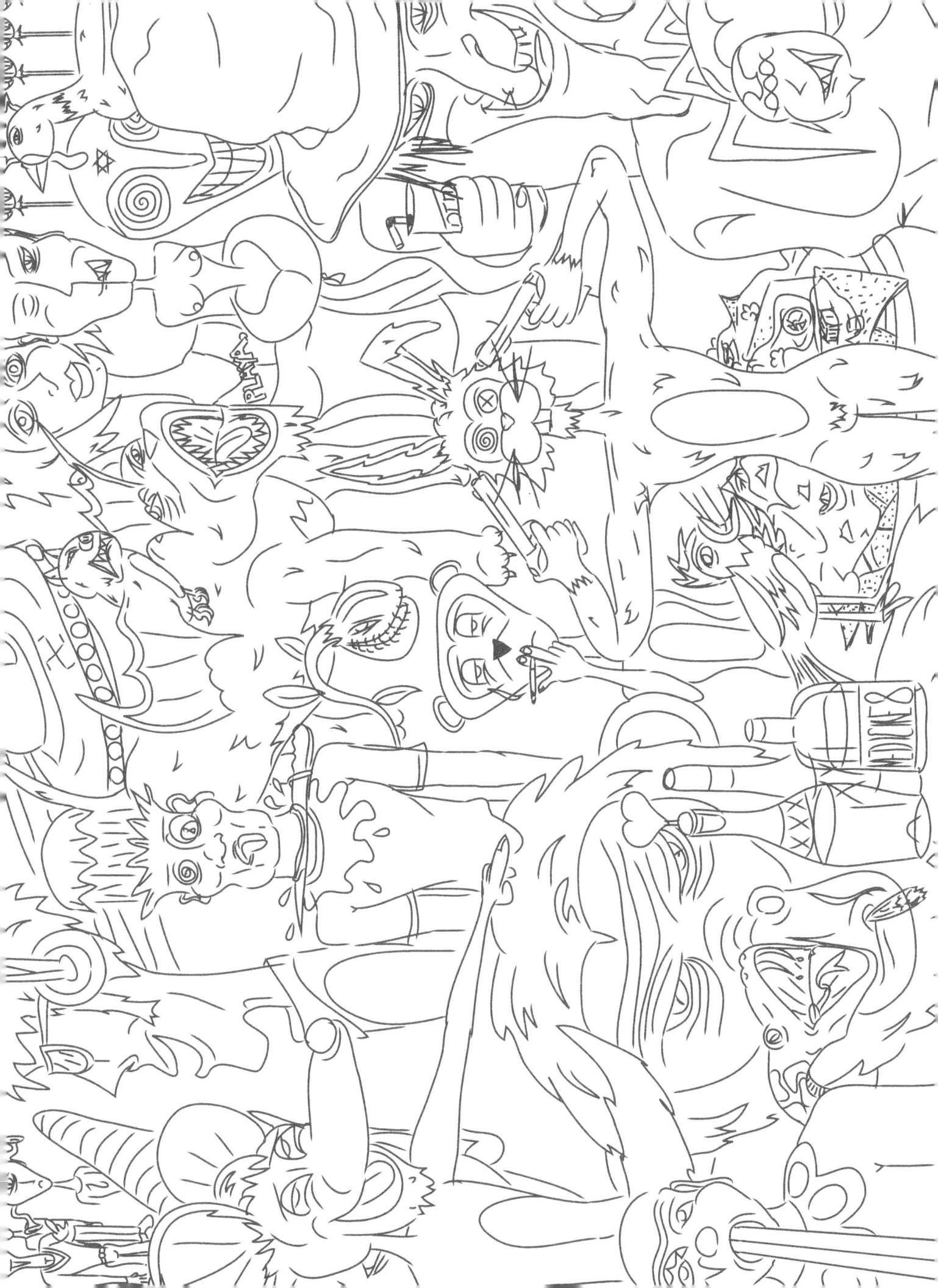

Title: Bunny
2016

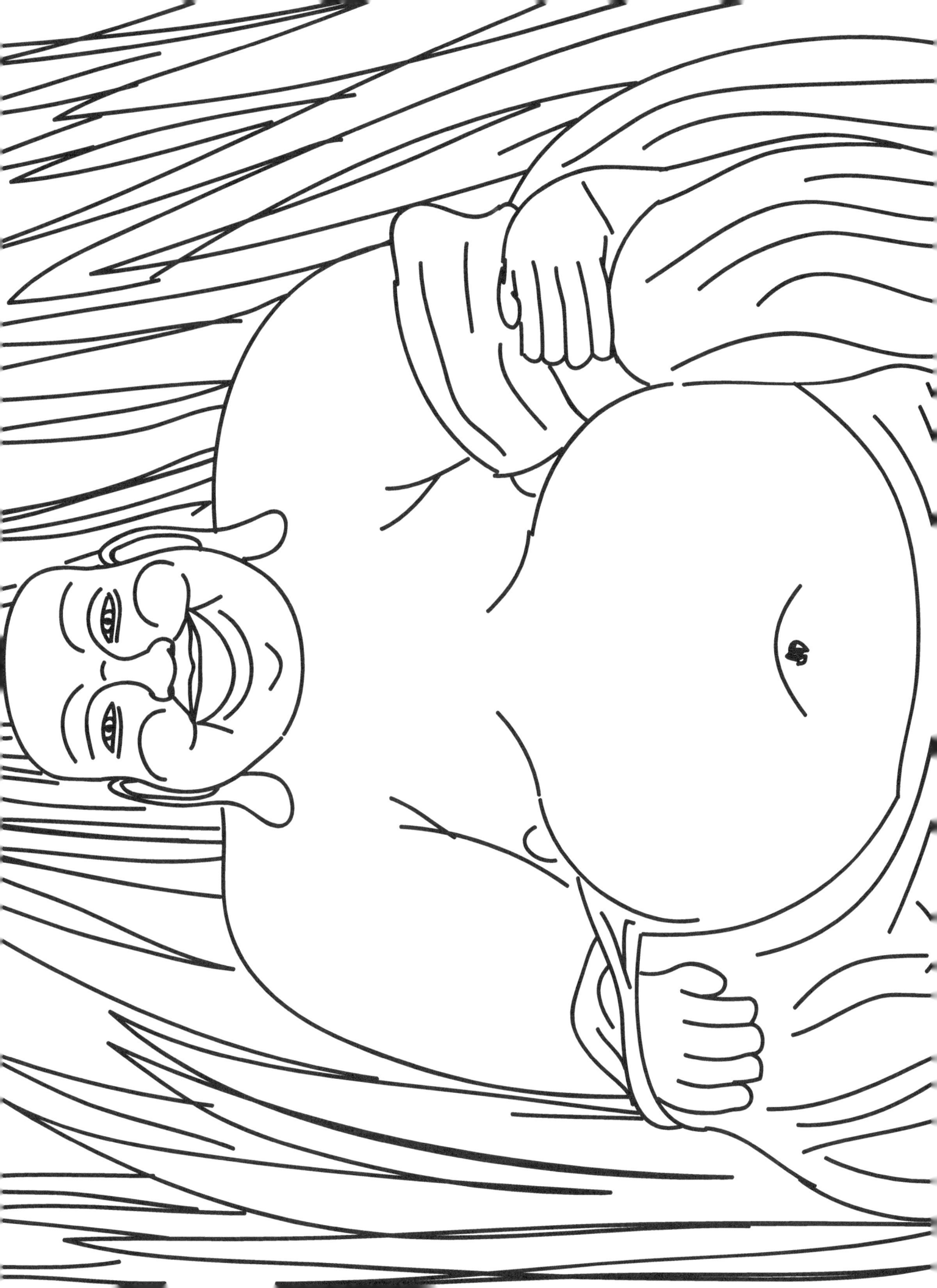

Title: Bud
2014

MULTI-PAGE ARTWORK

Title: 2Face

2014

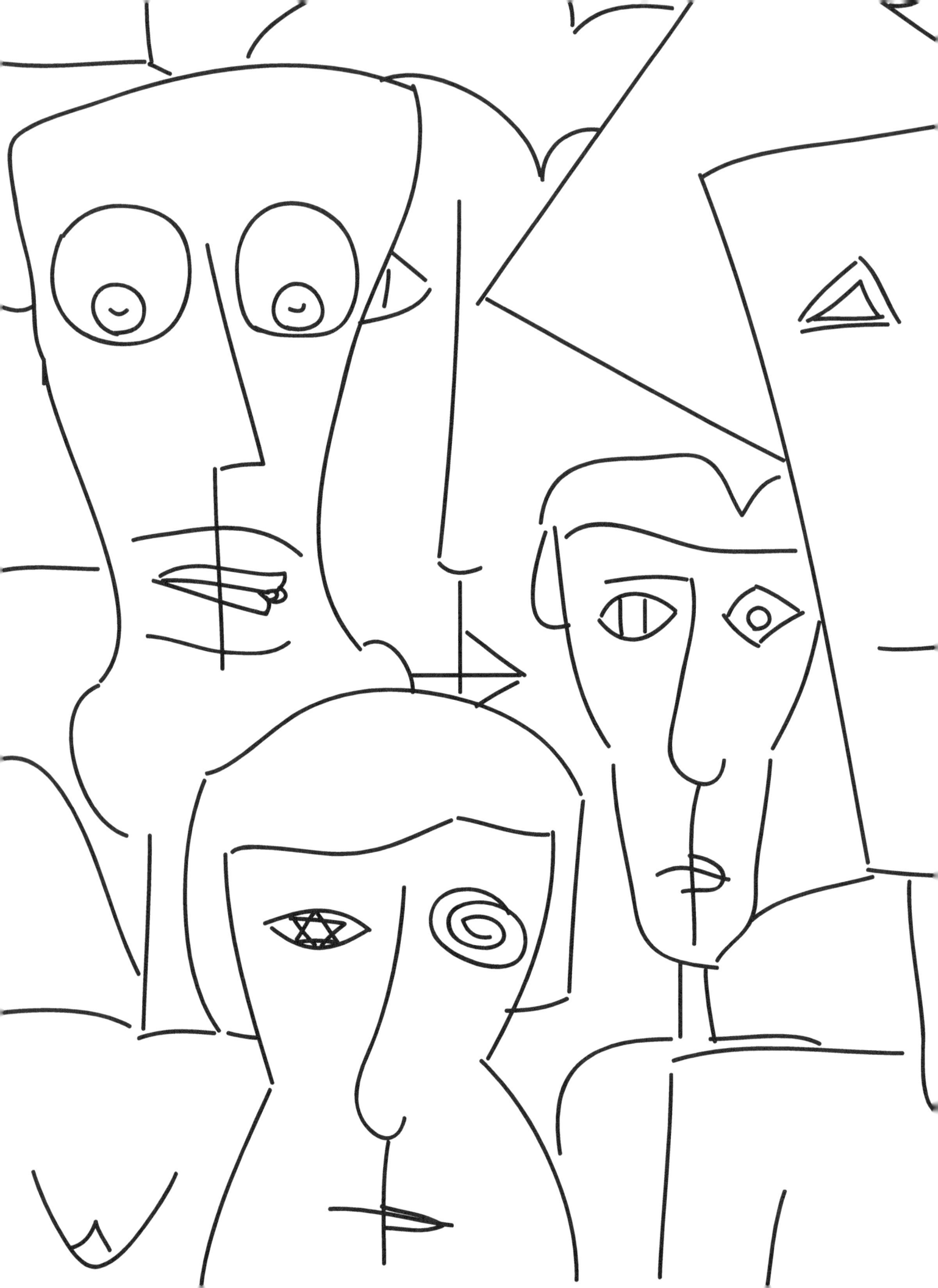

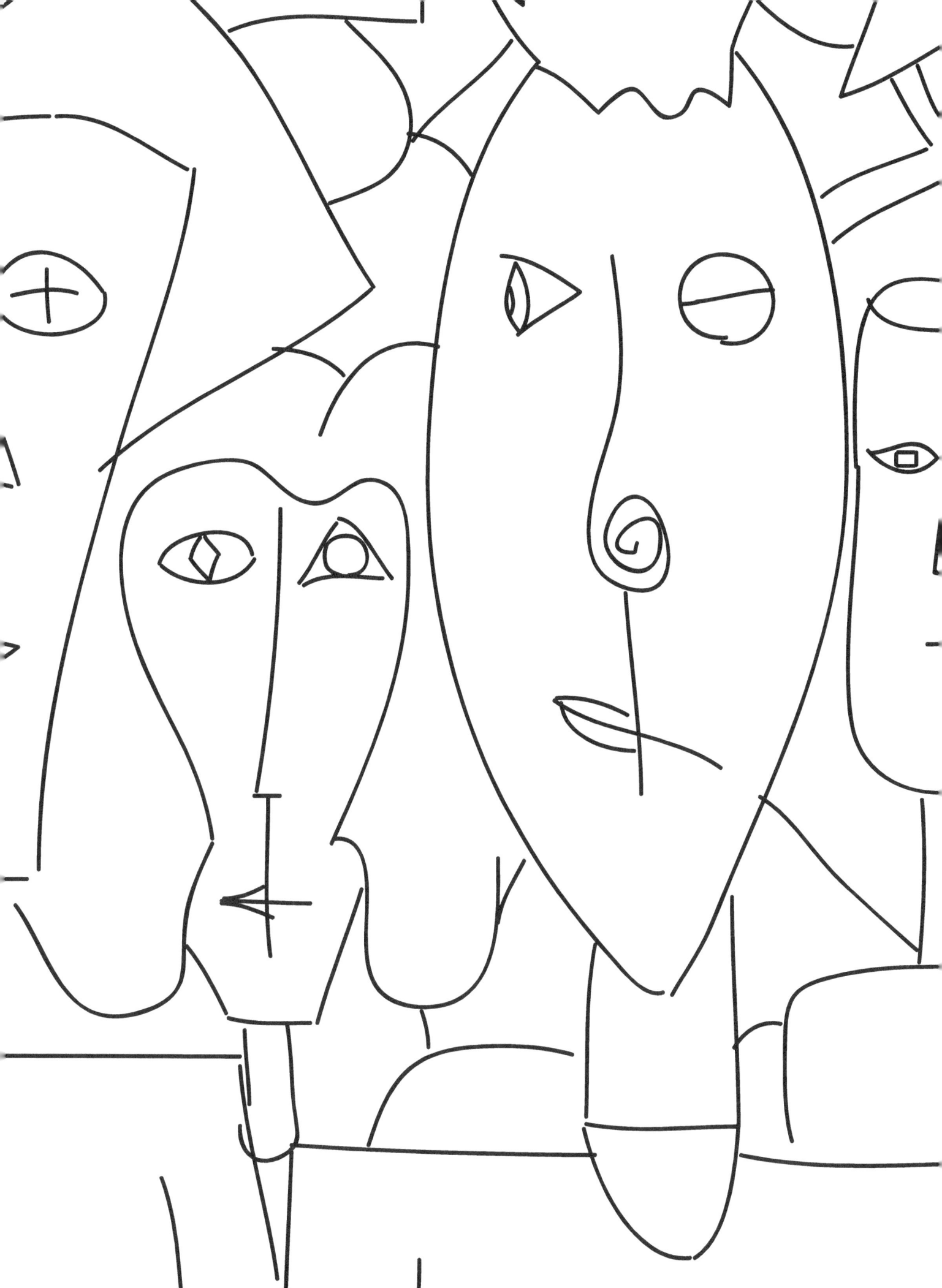

MULTI-PAGE ARTWORK

Title: 2Face

2014

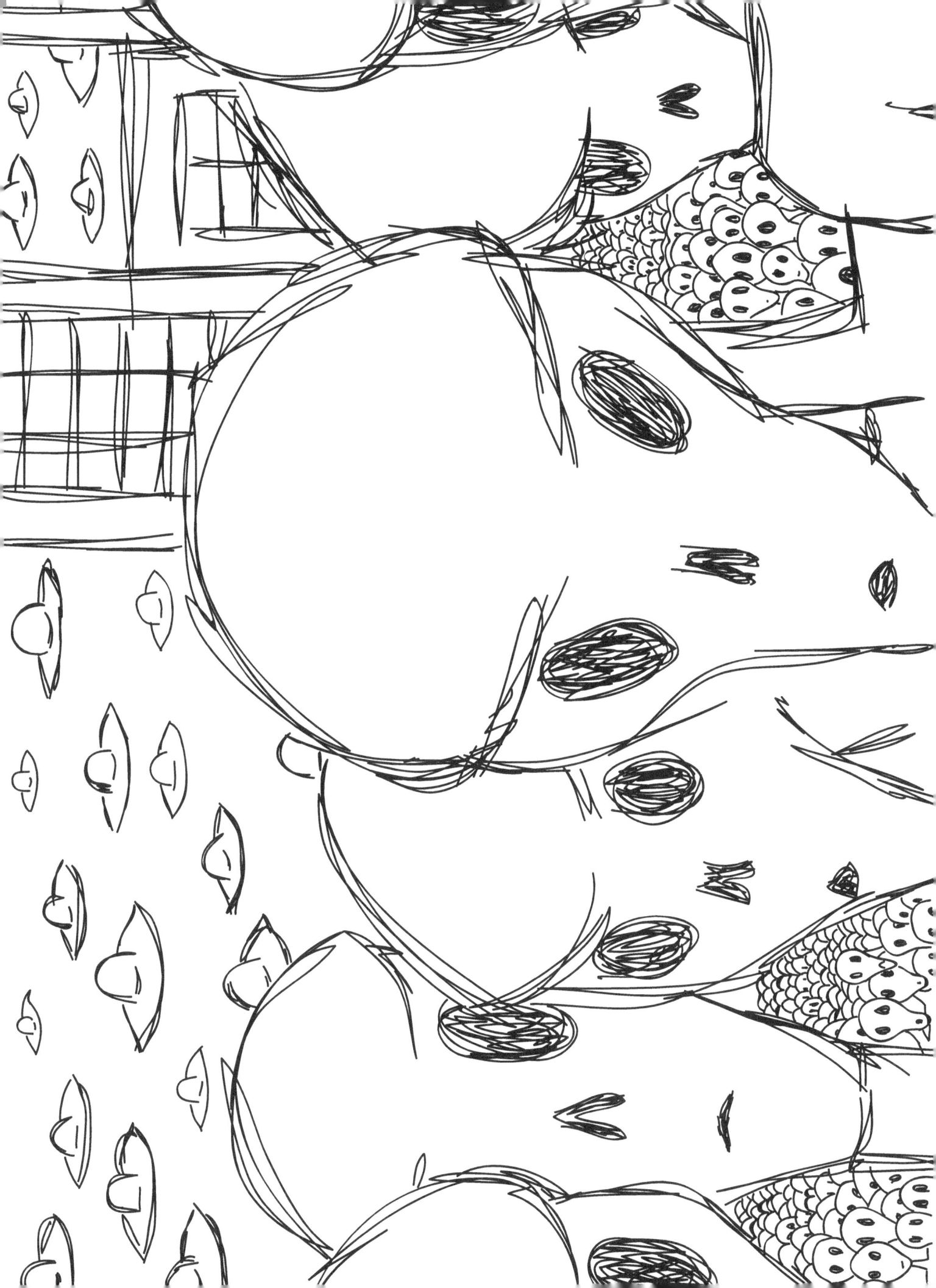

Title: AZ
2014

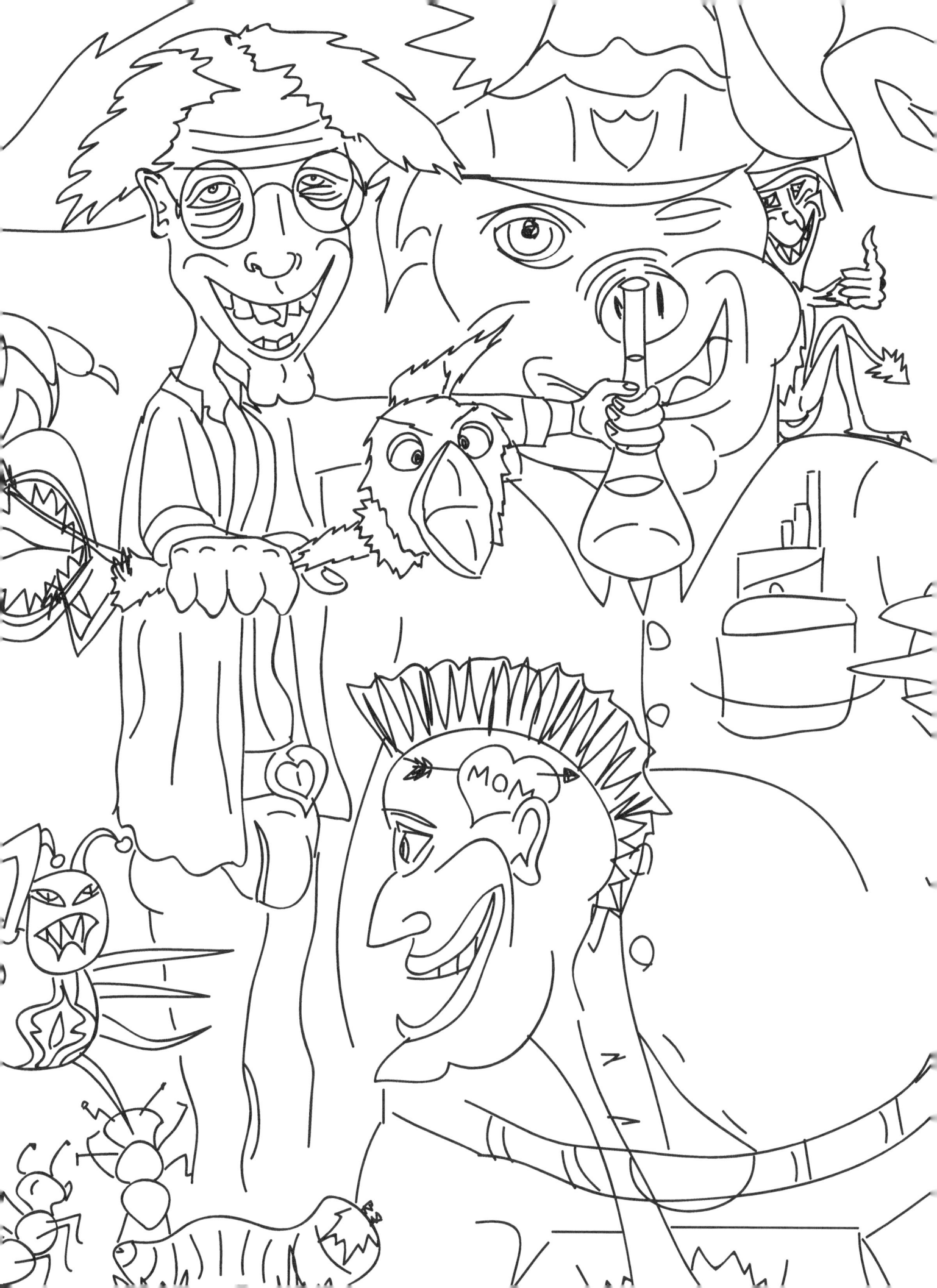

Title: Wrandom
2016

MULTI-PAGE ARTWORK

Title: Gas
2014

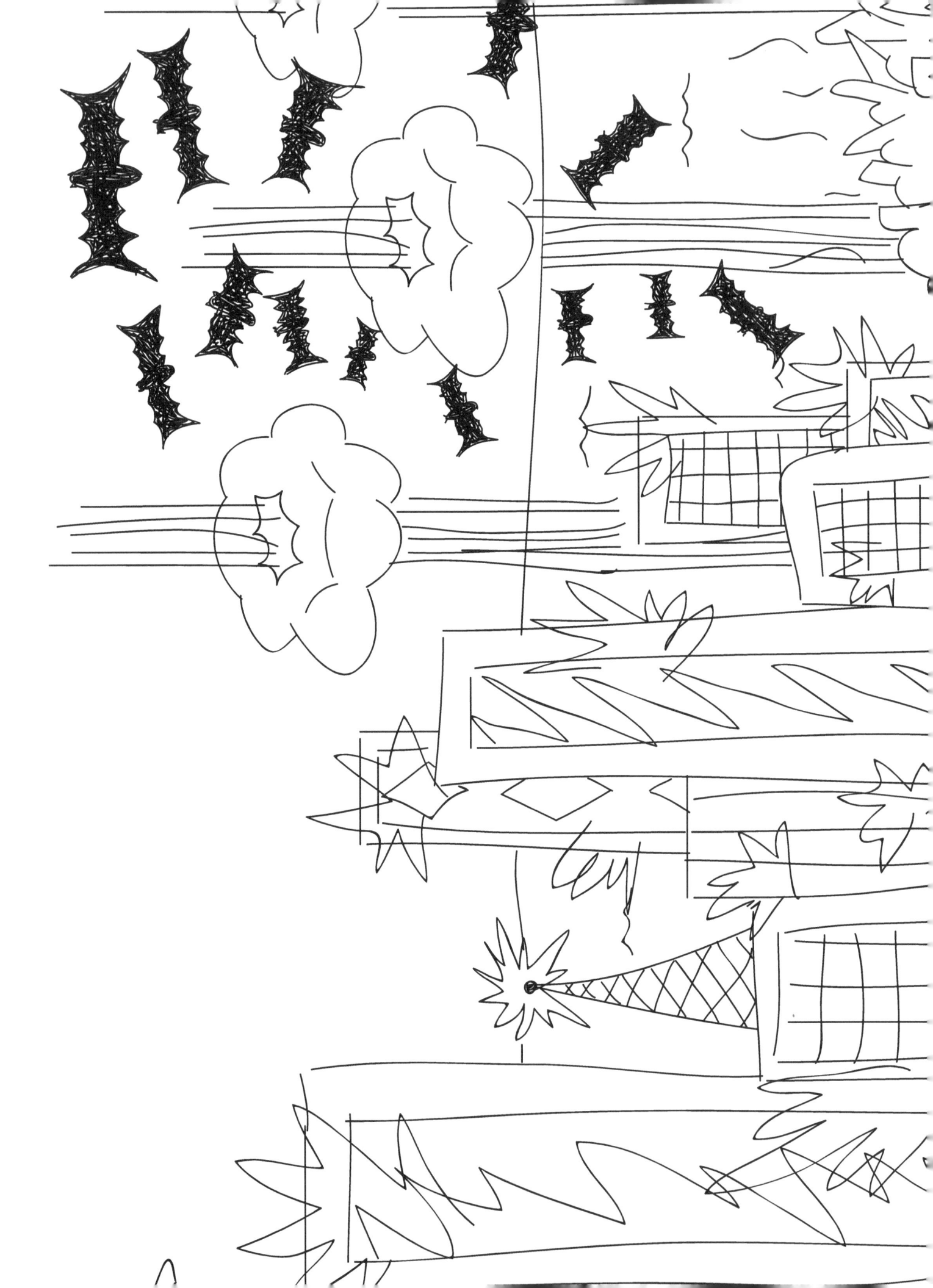

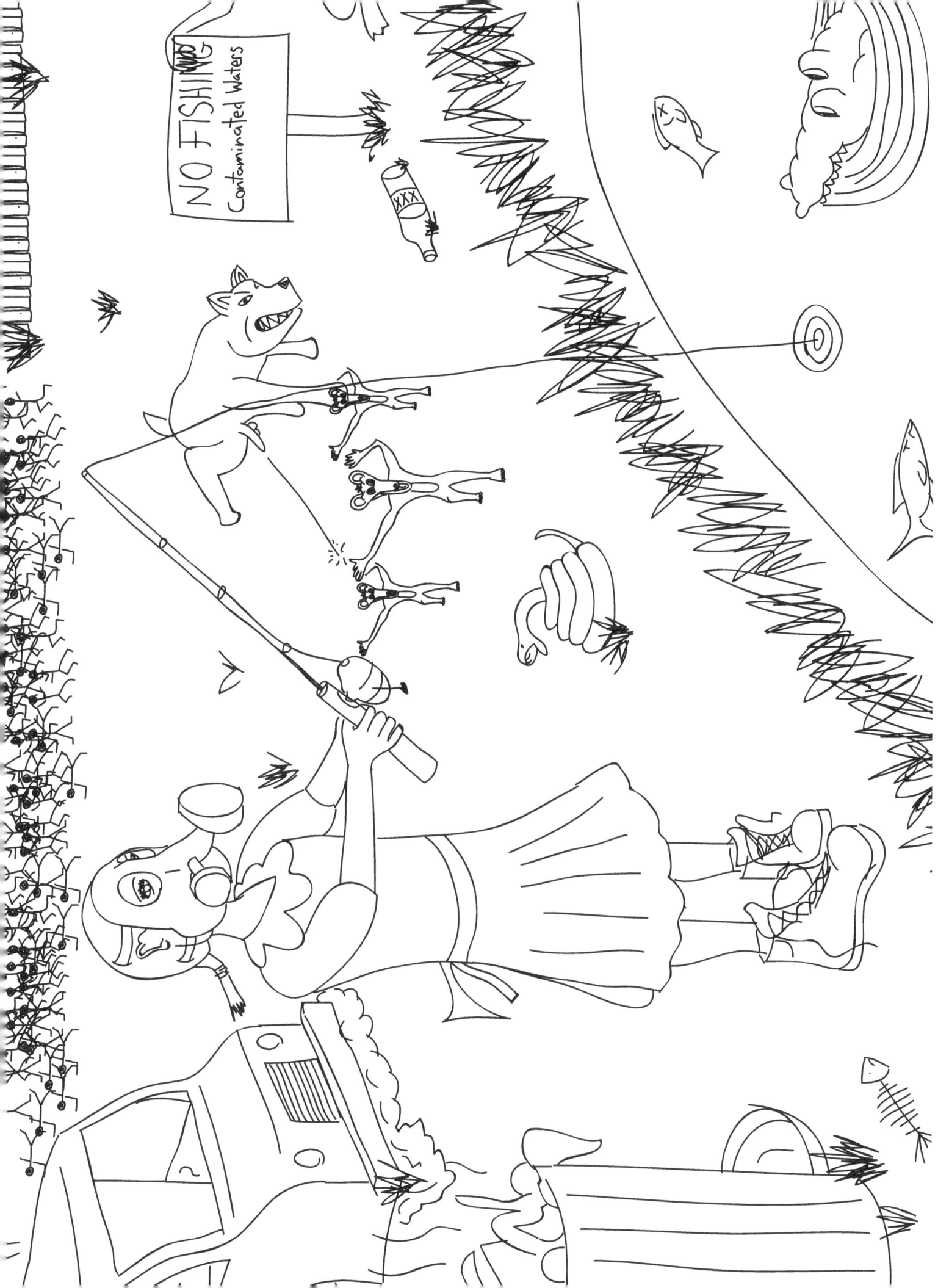

MULTI-PAGE ARTWORK

Title: Gas
2014

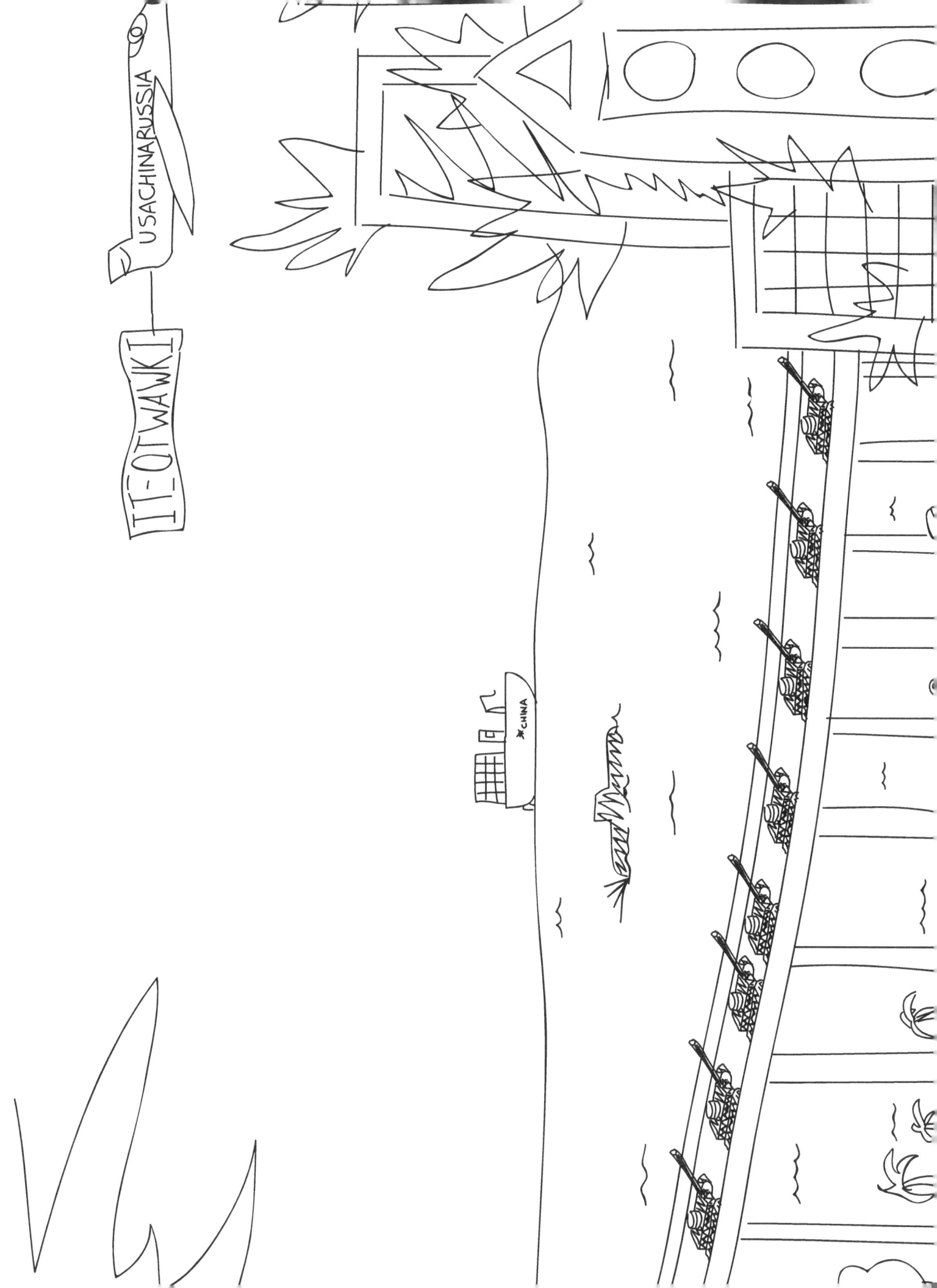

MULTI-PAGE ARTWORK

Title: Gas
2014

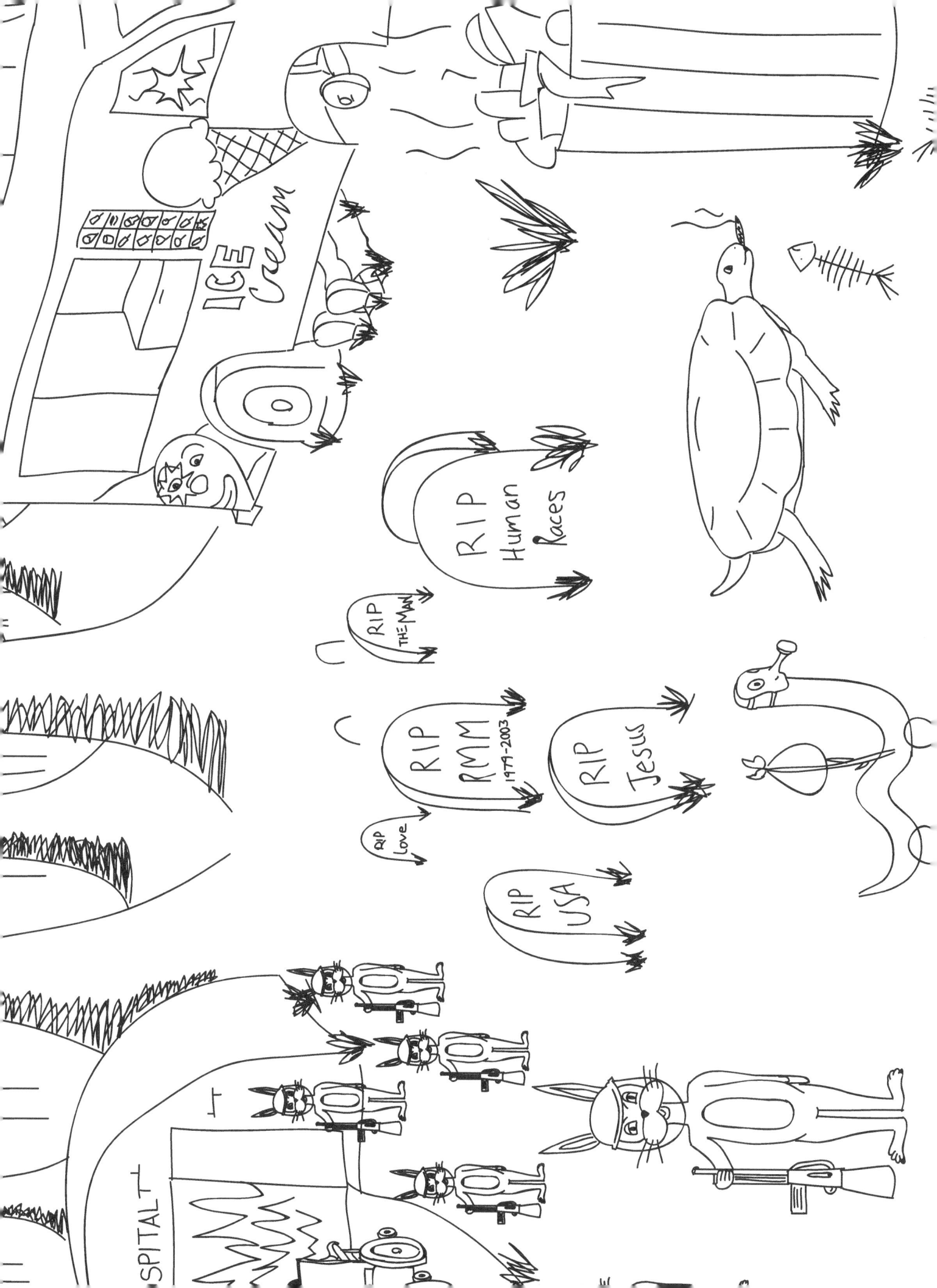

MULTI-PAGE ARTWORK

Title: Gas
2014

MULTI-PAGE ARTWORK

Title: Chill
2014

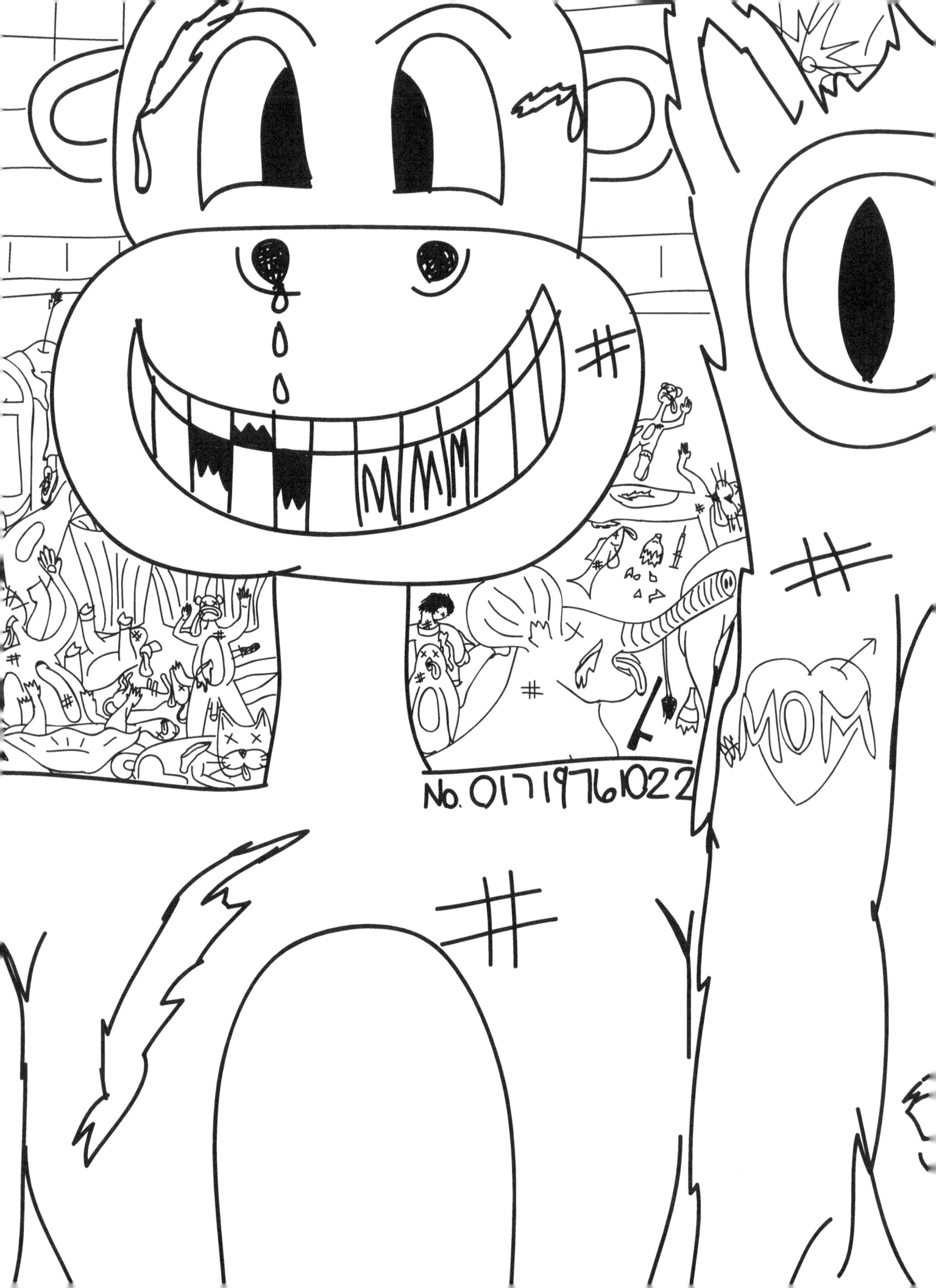

No. 0171976 1022

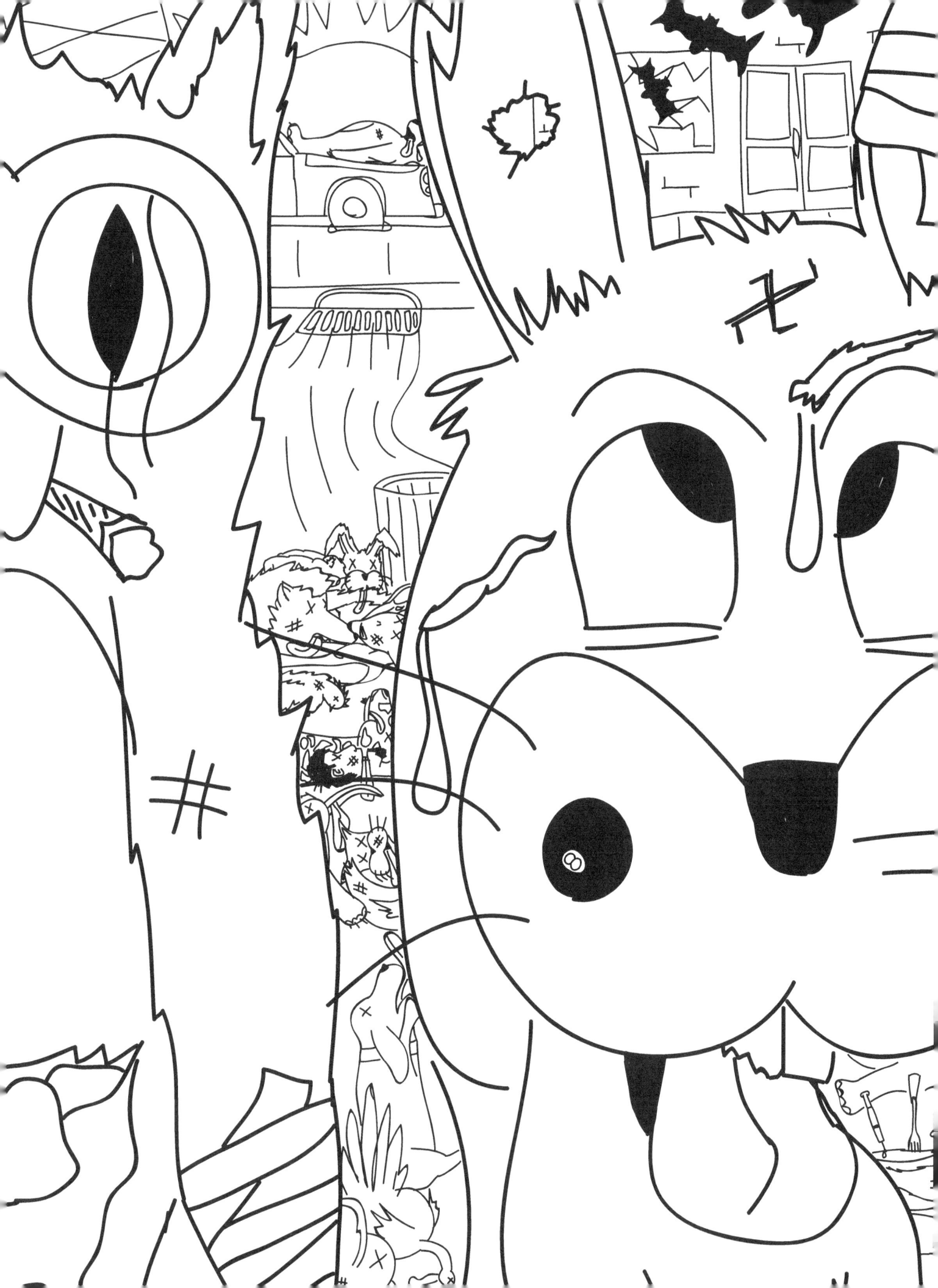

MULTI-PAGE ARTWORK

Title: Chill
2014

MULTI-PAGE ARTWORK

Title: Surf
2014

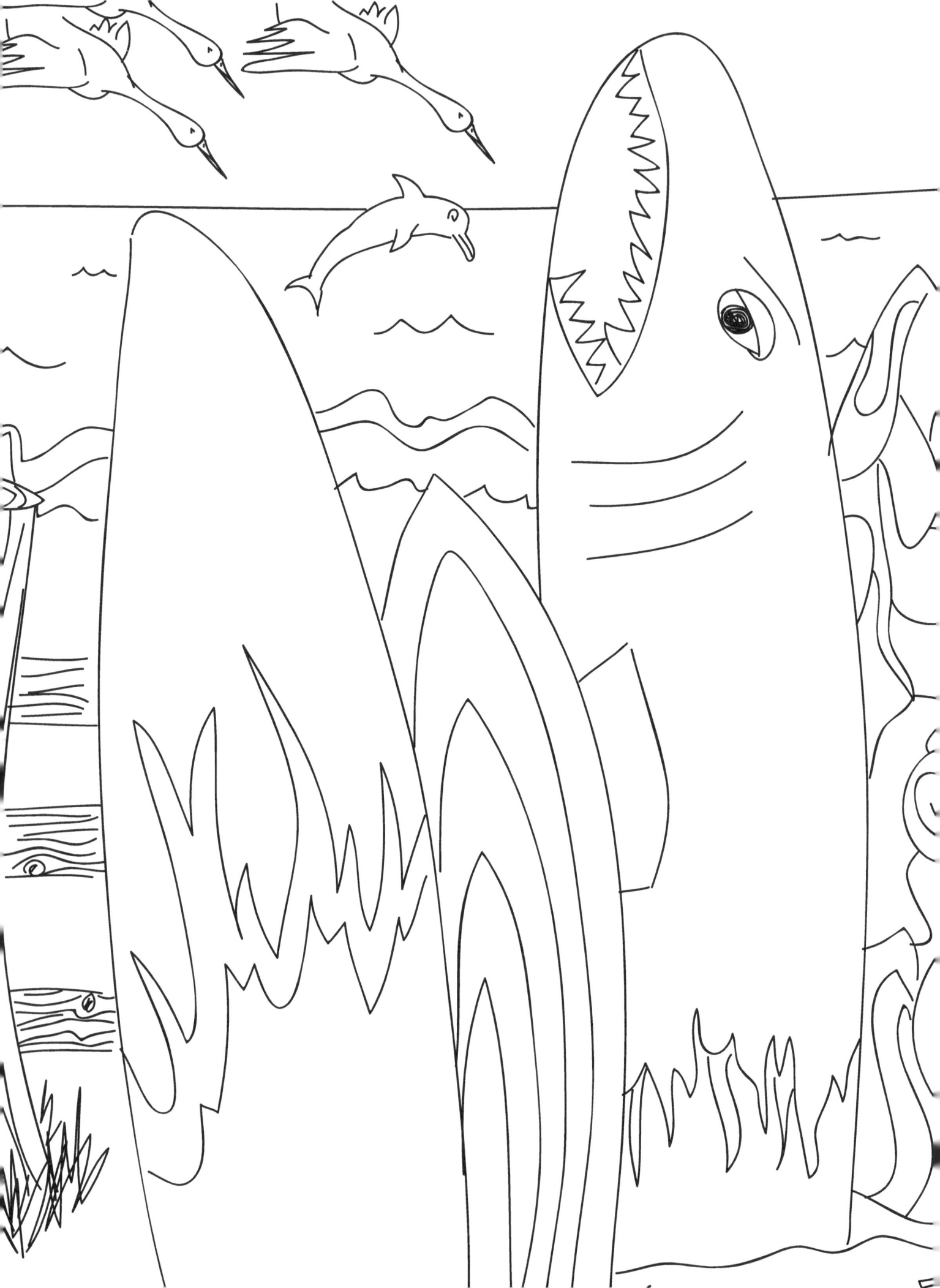

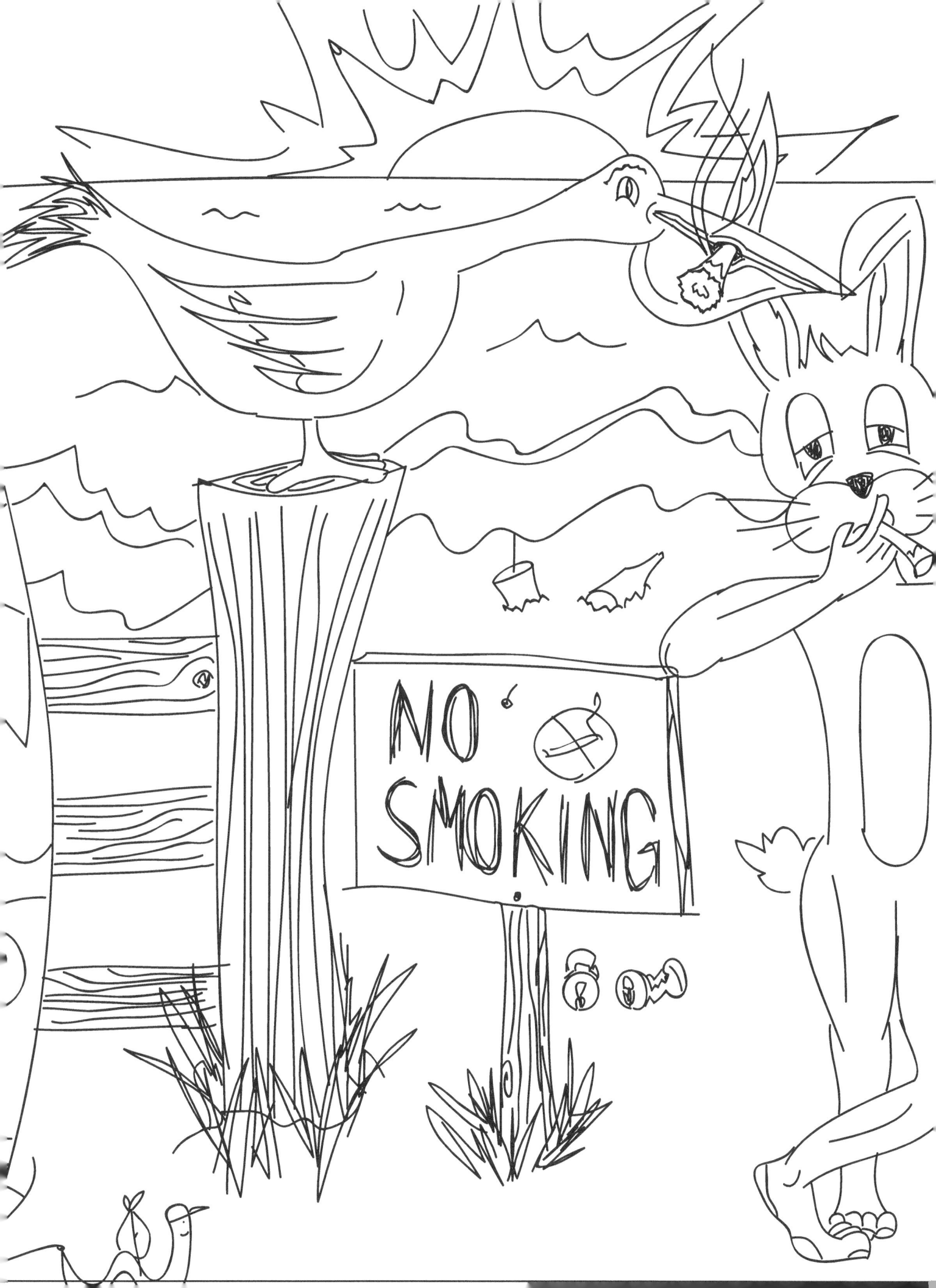

MULTI-PAGE ARTWORK

Title: Surf

2014

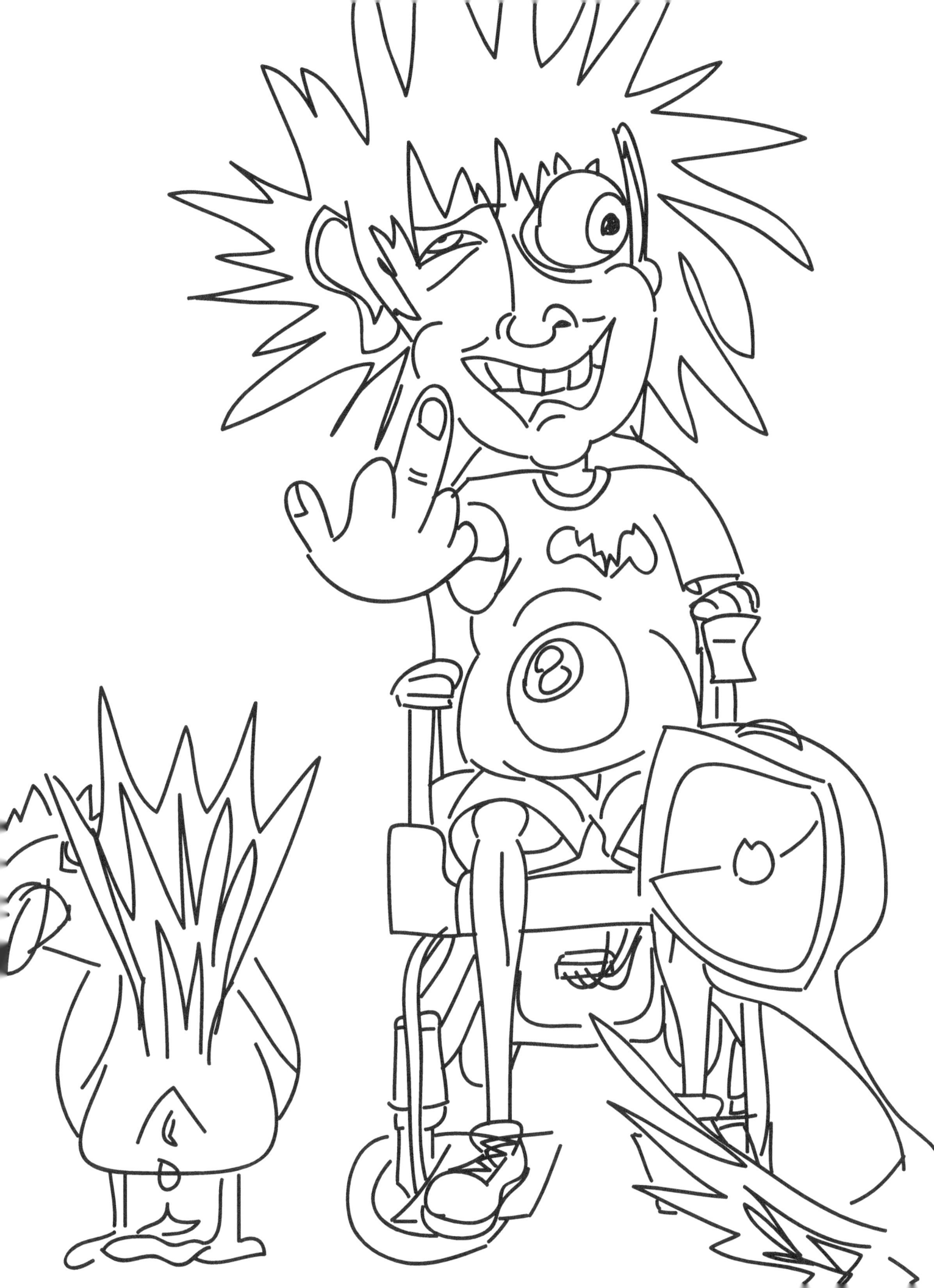

Title: That's Life
2016

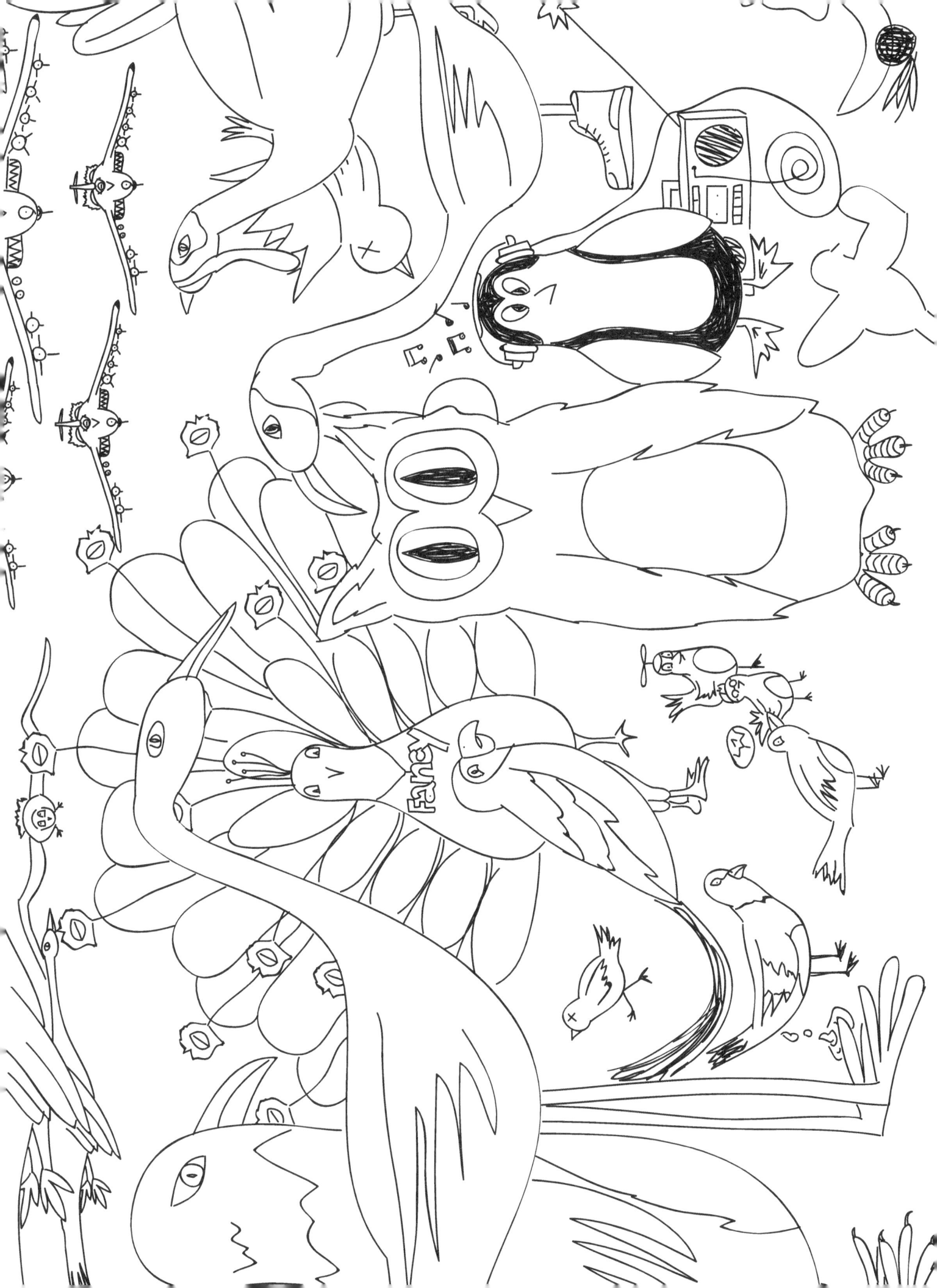

Title: Bird
2014

MULTI-PAGE ARTWORK

Title: Social Security

2014

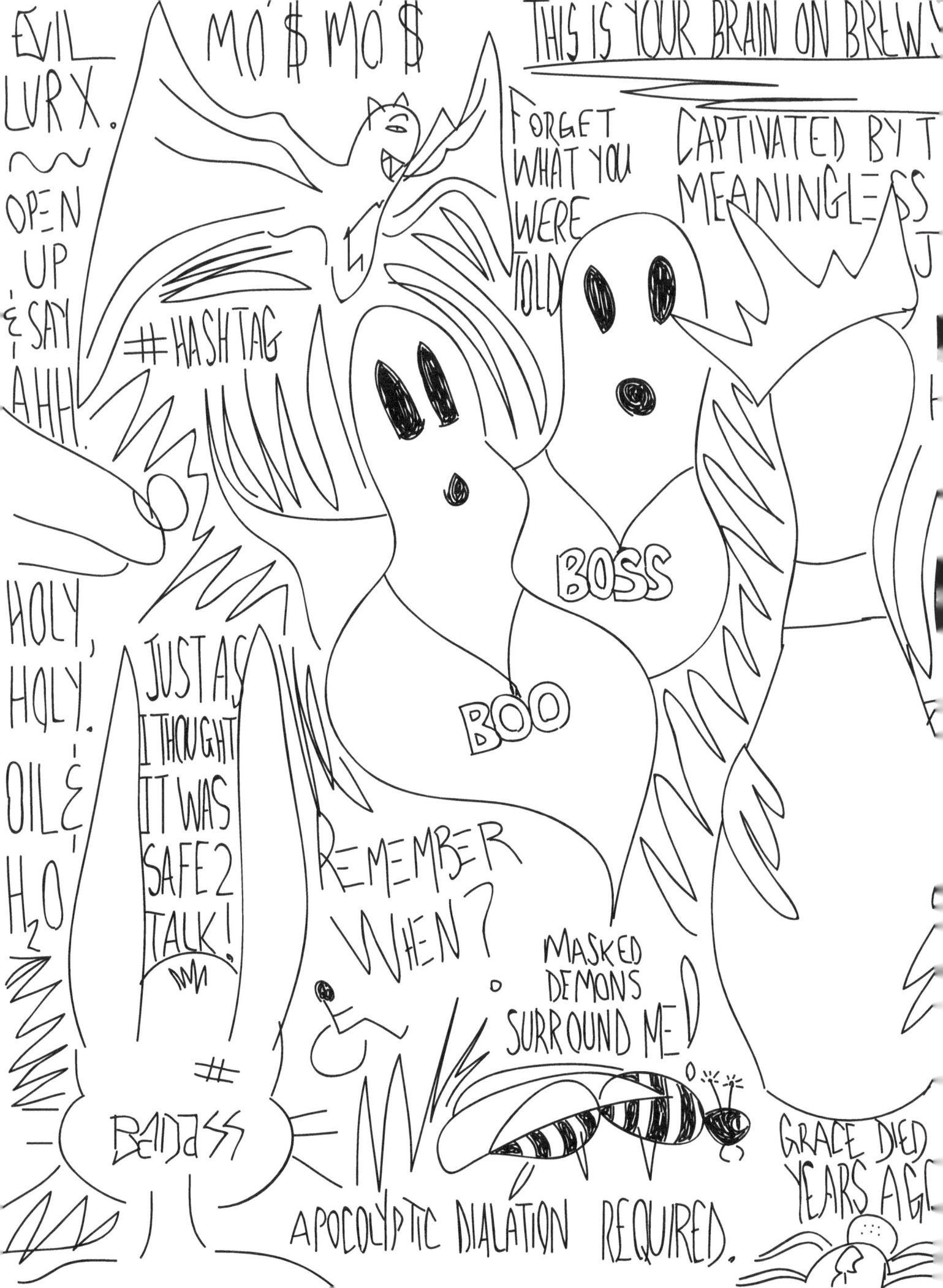

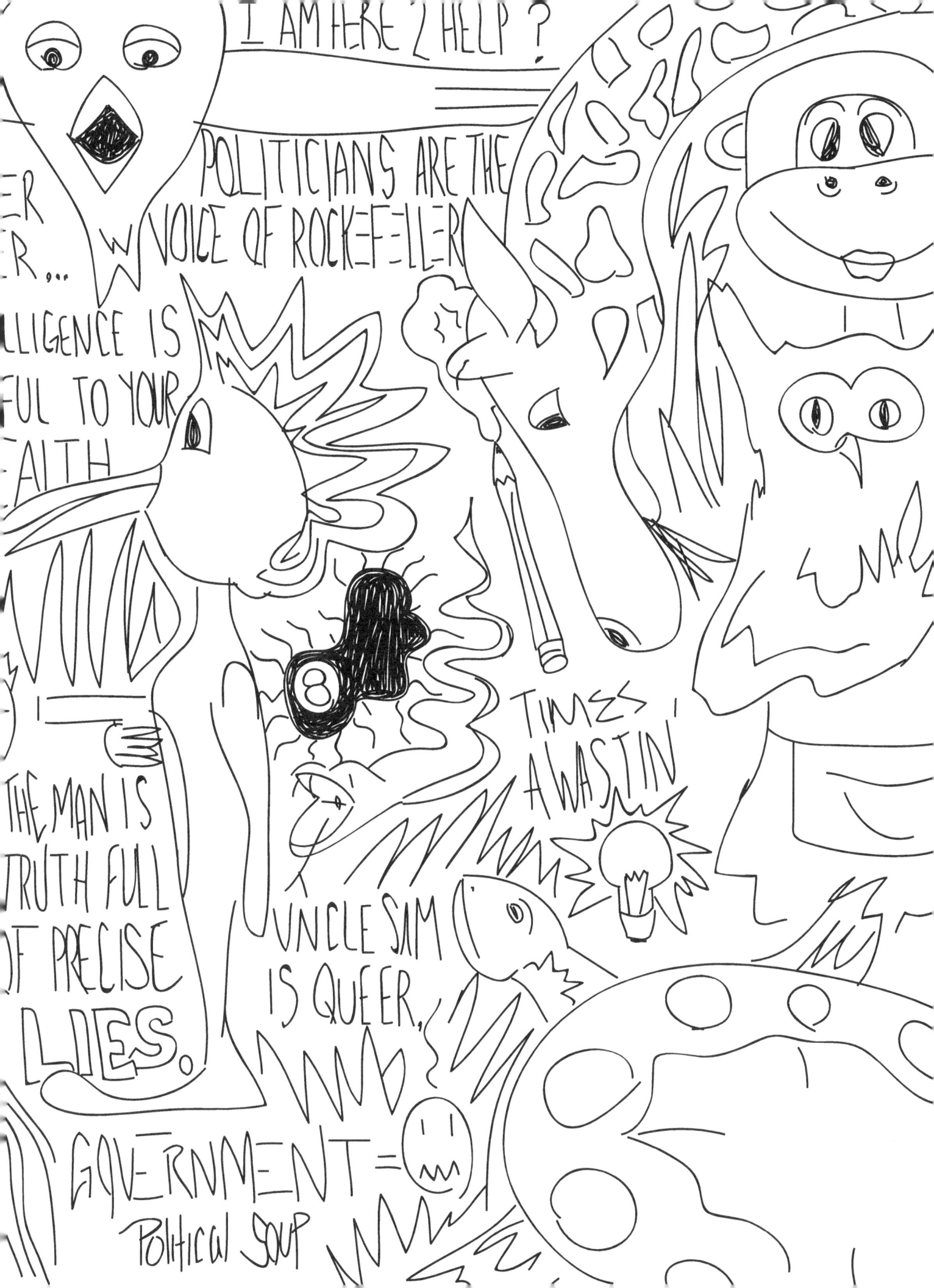

MULTI-PAGE ARTWORK

Title: Social Security

2014

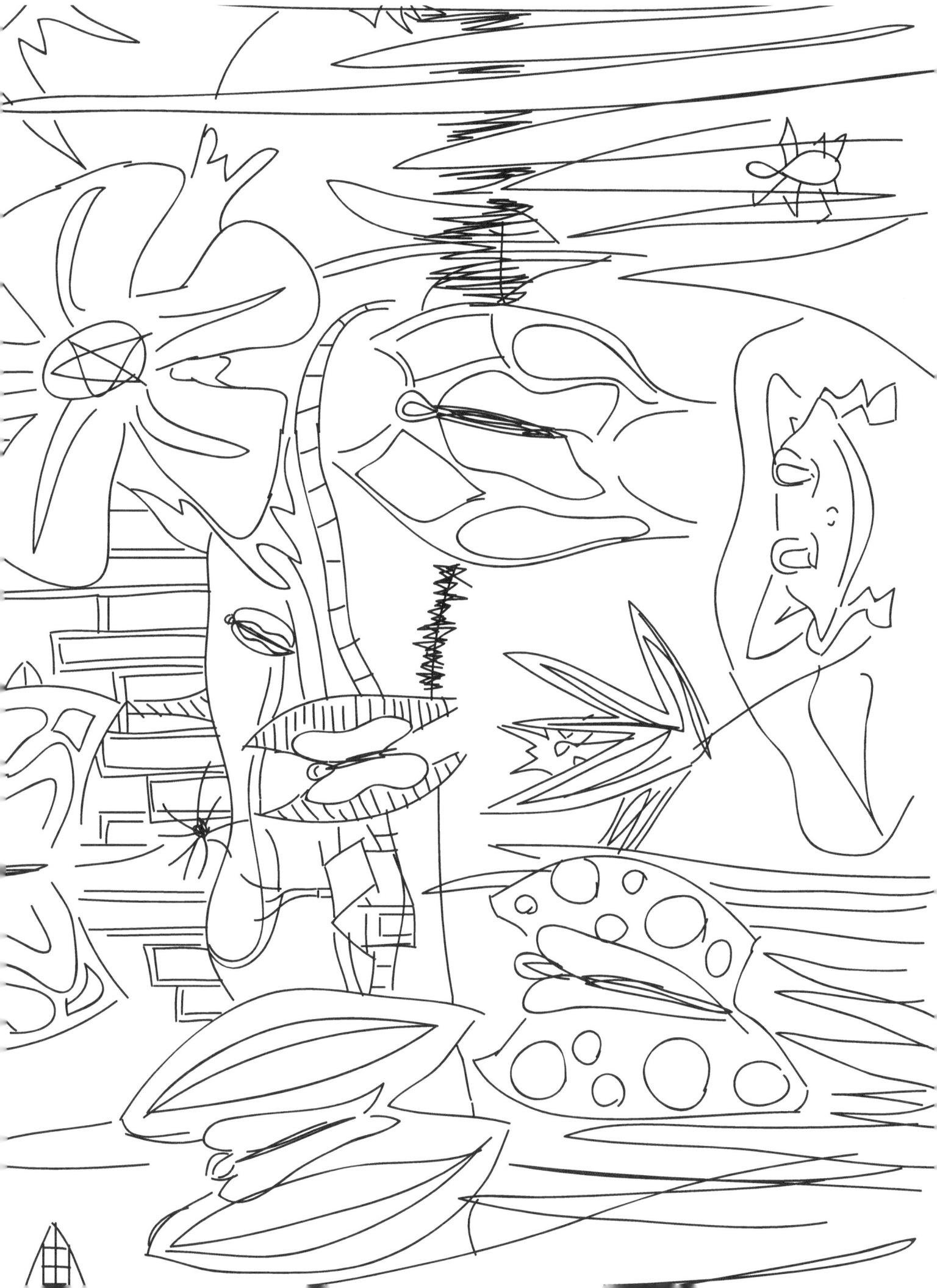

Title: Butters
2014

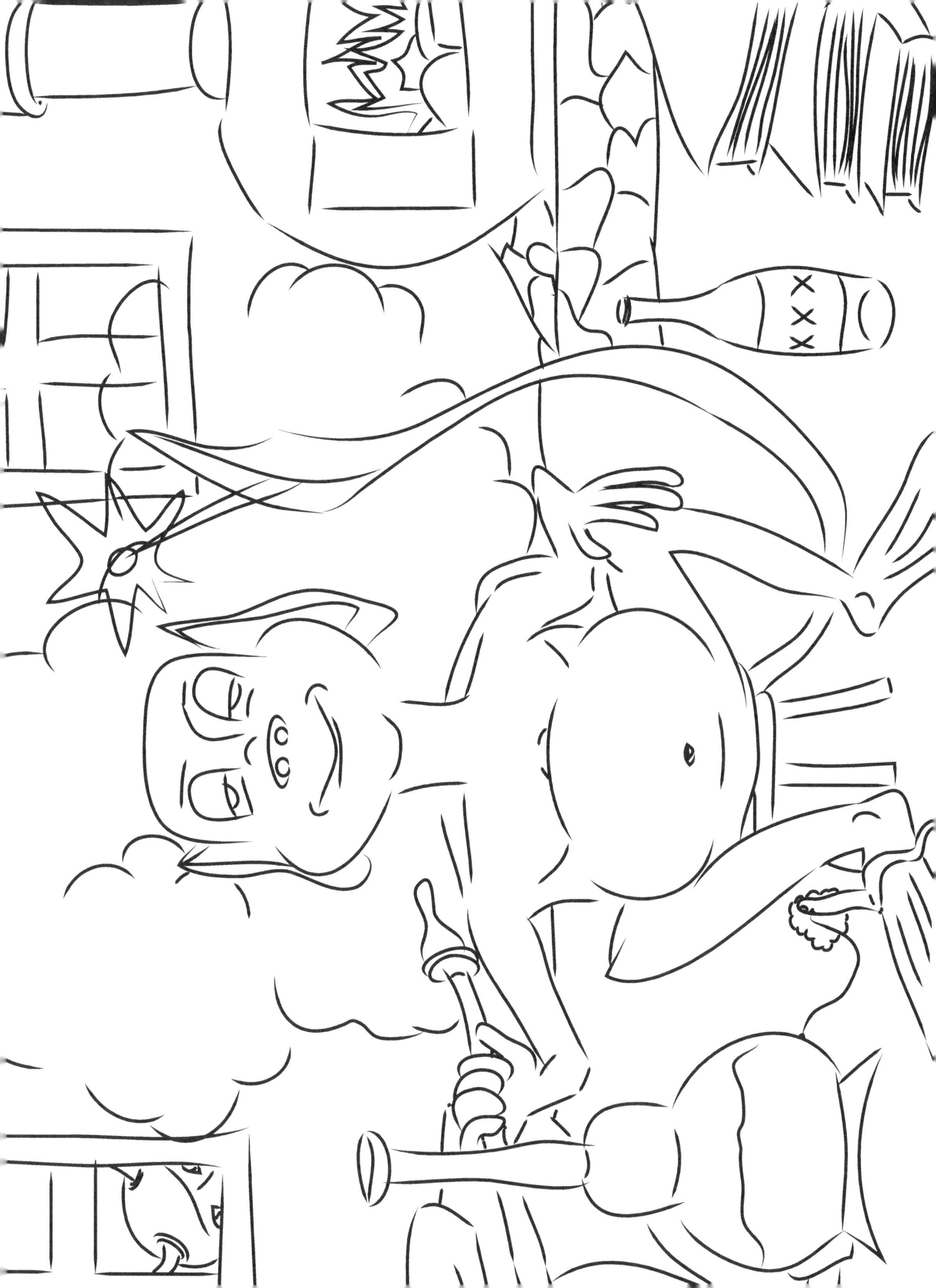

Title: Clyde
2014

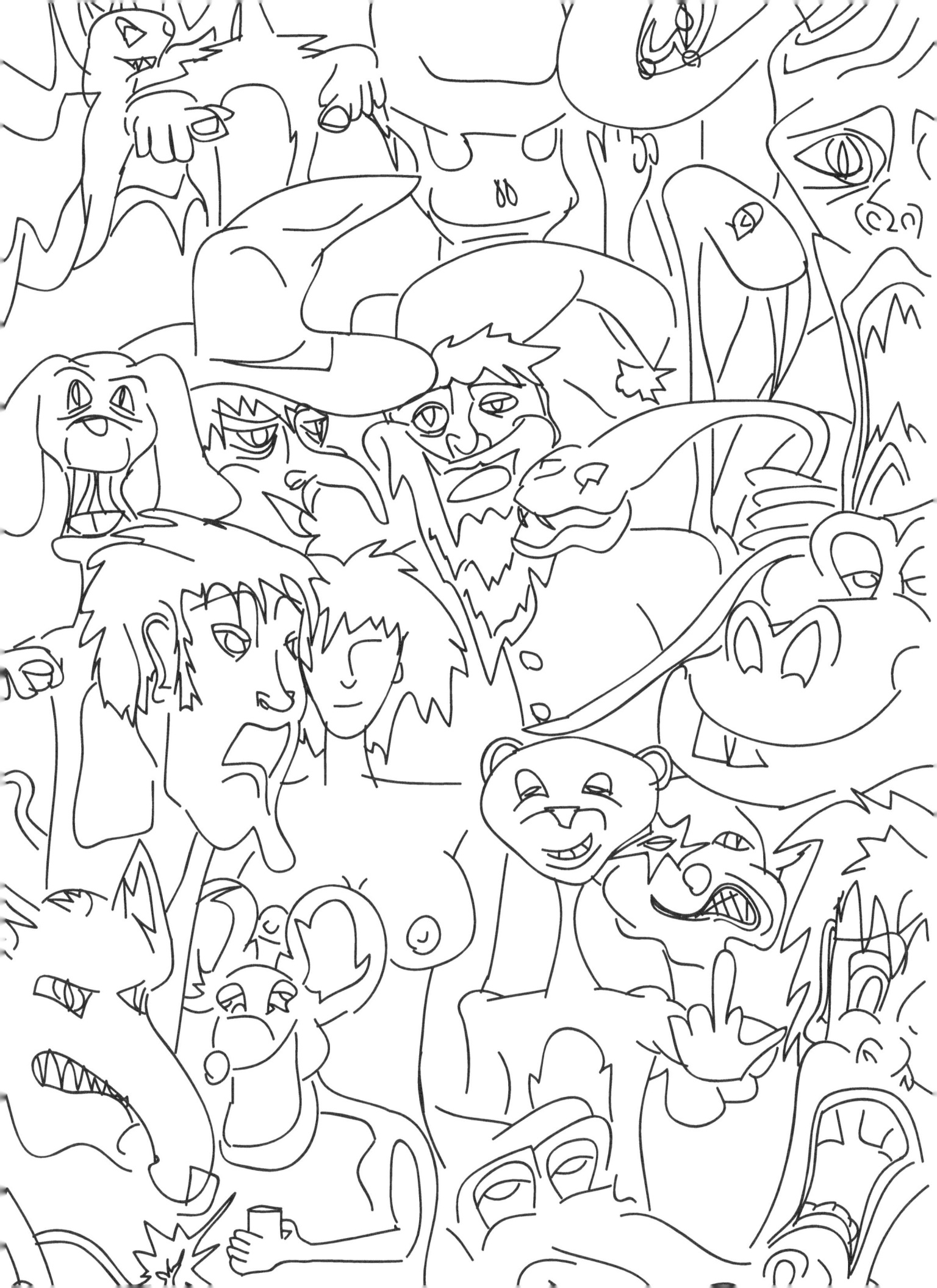

Title: Truth
2015